Britain in the Past

The Romans

Moira Butterfield

W
FRANKLIN WATTS
LONDON•SYDNEY

Franklin Watts
First published in 2015 by the Watts Publishing Group

Editor: Sarah Ridley
Editor in chief: John C. Miles
Series designer: Jane Hawkins
Art director: Peter Scoulding
Picture research: Diana Morris

Picture credits:
The Trustees of the British Museum: 27. Anthony Brown/Dreamstime: 20. Ian Dagnell/Alamy: 14. Andrew Emptage/Dreamstime: 8. Paris Franz/Alamy: 15. Johnbod/CC Wikimedia: 5. Mar Photographics/Alamy: 22. Andrew Michael/Alamy: 24tl. Jeff Morgan 10/Alamy: front cover. Stephen Mulcahey/Alamy: 4. Museum of London: 11, 12, 13, 16, 17, 23t, 23b. National Museum Wales: 19b. Photograph by Mike Peel (www.mikepeel.net)/ CC Wikimedia: 29. Photogenes: 9b. Portable Antiquities/CC Wkimedia.: 10. Roman Baths and Pump Room, Bath: 21cr. Mark Salter/ Alamy: 1, 7. Skyscan PL/Alamy: 6, 28. St Albans Museums Service: 18. UK City Images/Alamy: 25. Vindolanda: 9t. Warrington Museum & Art Gallery: 24cr. Wellcome Library /CC Wikimedia: 21cl. Edward Westmacott/Dreamstime: 19t. World History Archive/Alamy: 26.

Dewey number: 941

Hardback ISBN: 978 1 4451 4054 4
Library eBook ISBN: 978 1 4451 4055 1

Printed in China

Franklin Watts
An imprint of
Hachette Children's Group
Part of The Watts Publishing Group
Carmelite House
50 Victoria Embankment
London EC4Y 0DZ

An Hachette UK Company
www.hachette.co.uk

www.franklinwatts.co.uk

Contents

Land in Britain!

Nearly 2,000 years ago, in 43 CE, a fleet of wooden ships carrying 50,000 Roman soldiers landed on the coast of Kent to take over Britannia – their name for Britain.

Friend or enemy?

Before the Romans came, Celtic people known as Britons ruled different parts of Britain. When the Romans arrived, some local leaders welcomed them in and agreed to work with them. Other Celtic tribes fought the Romans to the death.

If you were Roman...

If you were a Roman soldier, you needed to be careful not to wander into lonely spots where enemy Celts lurked. They liked to take home the heads of Romans as trophies!

Roman soldiers were well trained and well equipped.▼

Look!

Celtic leaders wore gold torcs to show their importance to their own people and the invading Romans. The torcs were similar to the Great Torc (below), found in Snettisham, Norfolk.

Face the Celts

The local Celts were frightening to meet in battle. Their fiercest warriors fought naked except for a sword belt and a twisted metal necklace called a torc. They painted strange blue patterns on their skin and screamed as they charged into battle. They were brave but badly organised, and no match for the highly trained Roman army.

Here comes Claudius

The Roman Empire was based in Rome, Italy. In 43 CE it was ruled by Emperor Claudius, who arrived in Britannia a few weeks after his army. He rode into Camulodunum (now called Colchester) on the back of an elephant to accept the surrender of tribal leaders. It took many years for the Romans to control southern Britain and they never conquered Scotland or Ireland.

March with the army

Ordinary Roman soldiers marched everywhere on foot, sometimes for up to 32 km (20 miles) or more a day. They were trained to always obey orders.

Big bases

The army had three permanent fortresses around Britain, at Chester, York and Caerleon in Wales. Some of the best fortress remains are in Caerleon, where you can see all sorts of things that the troops left behind. Roman soldiers marched from here to fight the Celts. It took 30 years for the Romans to take control of Wales.

If you were Roman...

Soldiers sometimes had time to relax. At Caerleon they could have a swim in the bathhouse (see p20) or watch a gladiator fight.

Caerleon fortress, showing the barracks where 5,000 soldiers slept. ▼

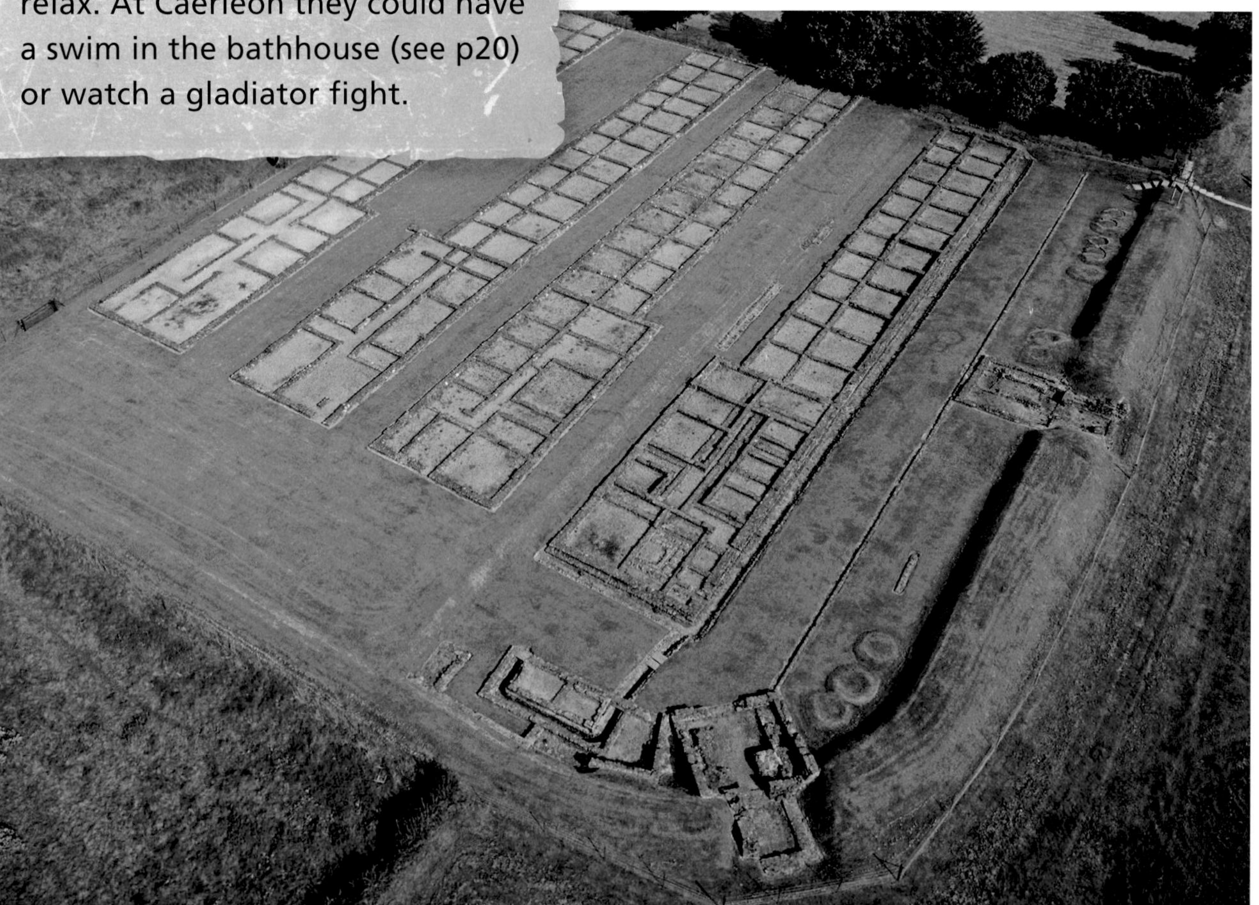

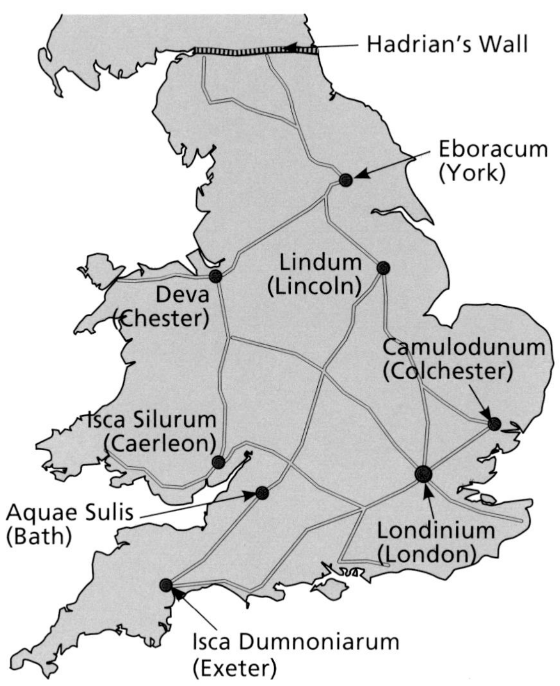

▲ This map shows Roman Britain, with some of the major towns and roads.

Overnight camping

Roman soldiers lived in forts, but when they were on the move they slept in tents made of animal skins. They protected their temporary camp by digging a ditch and piling up an earth wall around it. The wall was topped with wooden stakes that the soldiers carried with them. Soldiers took turns patrolling at night, watching out for trouble.

Roman roadworks

Roman soldiers built roads for the first time in Britain, laying down stones and digging drainage ditches on either side. The roads were made as straight as possible, so there were no hidden corners where enemies could hide. Some modern roads still run along old Roman routes – for instance, the Fosse Way still runs from Lincoln to Exeter.

If you were Roman...

If you were an ordinary Roman soldier you would take orders from a centurion, who wore a horse-hair crest on his helmet to show his rank (see below). If you angered him he might hit you with a wooden stick he carried, called a *vitis*.

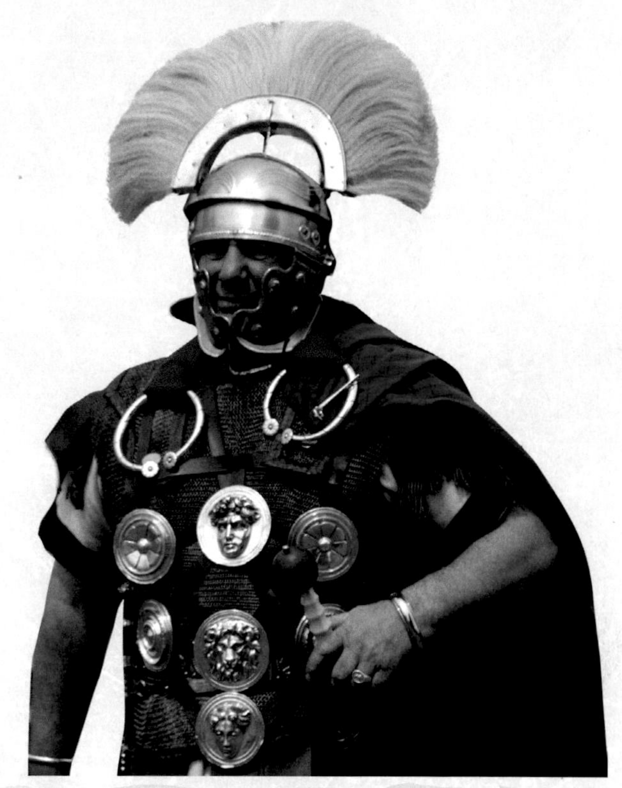

Guard the frontier

Once southern Britain was under control, Roman soldiers were sent to build a wall stretching across what is now northern England. Today we call it Hadrian's Wall after the Emperor Hadrian who ordered it to be built in 122 CE.

Why the wall?

The stone and turf wall was built to reinforce the northern frontier of the Roman Empire. It stretched for 117 km across the country and was dotted with towers and mini forts manned by troops. The wall kept out the Picts, tribes who lived to the north.

If you were Roman...

If you were a locally born male you could join the Roman army as an auxiliary. The army would especially welcome you if you had good horseriding or archery skills. Maybe you could become a cavalry soldier, firing arrows as you rode.

Finds around the forts

Behind the wall there were big forts for hundreds of troops. You can visit two of these sites at Housesteads and Vindolanda in Northumbria. Lots of Roman objects have been found there, including weapons, jewellery and shoes. Villages grew up around the forts for local families as well as soldiers.

Look!

In 2014 the first Roman wooden toilet seat ever found was discovered in Vindolanda. Stone or marble seats have been found before, but never wood. Wooden toilet seats are warmer to the touch, so people would have appreciated them in the icy north!

Writing on the wall

Hundreds of fragments of Roman handwriting were discovered in a rubbish pit at Vindolanda. They are the oldest pieces of handwriting ever found in the UK. The Latin writing was done in ink on thin pieces of wood, and the remains include letters from soldiers, merchants and ordinary men and women. One Roman lady sent her friend a birthday party invitation.

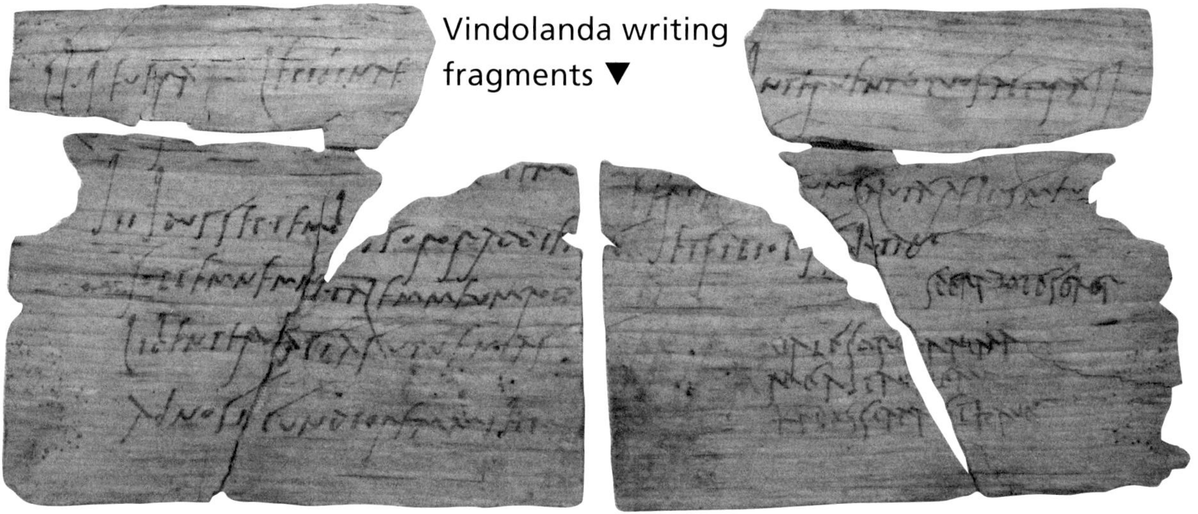

Vindolanda writing fragments ▼

Meet some people

After the invasion, local Britons gradually began to live like the Romans. Meanwhile people arrived in Britain from other parts of the Roman Empire.

Roman ranks

In the Roman world there were strict ranks in society.

- Roman men had full citizenship, which meant they had lots of rights and privileges.
- Roman women had fewer rights. For instance, they could not vote or hold posts in government.
- Beneath the citizens there were slaves who had no rights and were owned by their masters. They were either born into slavery or forced into it after being captured in battle. There were many slaves in Roman Britain, including some of the Celts defeated by the Romans.

If you were Roman...

If you were Roman you would own slaves to do your work for you. Any children born to your slaves would automatically belong to you, too. You could reward your slaves with freedom, but if a slave ran away, he or she could be hunted down and returned to you for punishment.

These Roman iron shackles stopped slaves from running away. ▼

The Romano-British

Over time, Britons began to wear Roman-style clothing and eat Roman-style food. They started to worship Roman gods, use Roman coins and buy Roman items for their homes, such as pots and glassware. We call these people the Romano-British. It seems they were keen to follow the lifestyle fashions that came from Rome.

Visitors from abroad

When it was at its largest, the Roman Empire stretched right across Europe and North Africa. People travelled around the Empire and some of them came to live in Britannia.

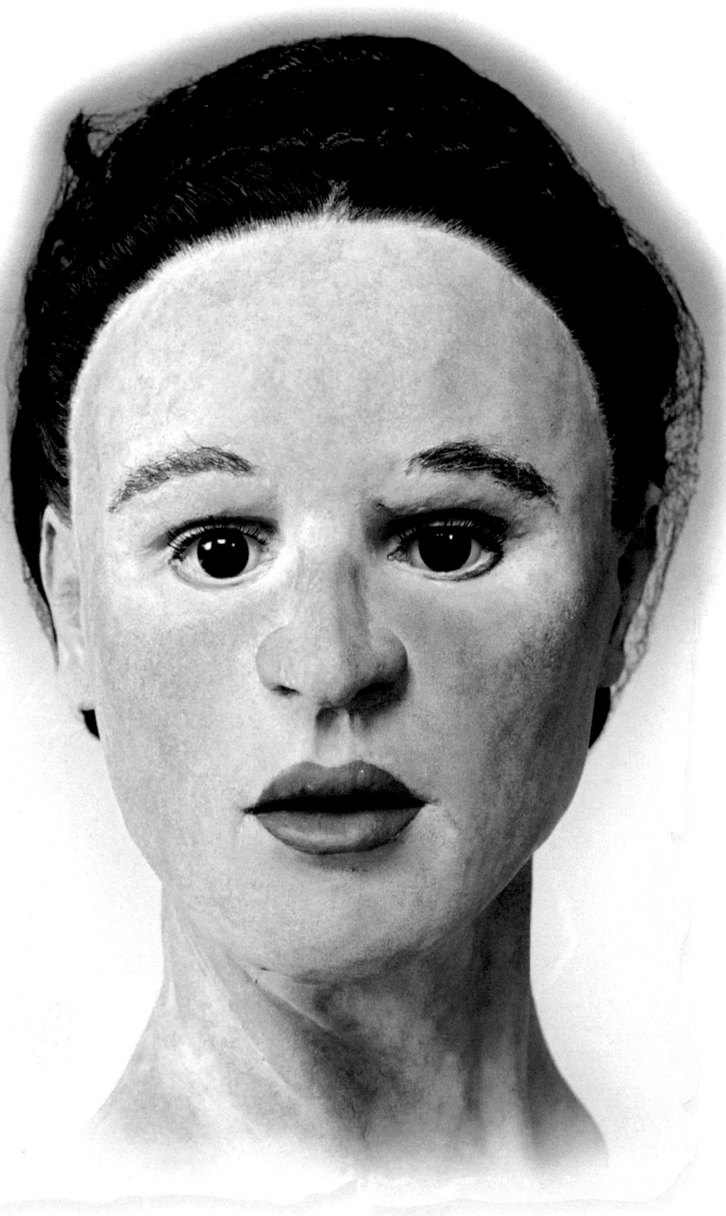

Look!

In 1999 archaeologists found the skeleton of a woman in a stone coffin in Spitalfields, London. Experts analysed the remains and discovered she was a young woman who died around 300–400 CE when she was around 20–25 years old. Evidence from her teeth revealed that she probably grew up in Spain. We don't know her name but experts have recreated her features based on her skull. You can see her coffin and this recreation of her face at the Museum of London.

Visit a villa

Ordinary Britons lived in wooden thatched homes, but wealthier people lived in stone town or country houses called villas.

On the farm

Wealthy landowners had country villas with their own farms. Romans kept bees in hives as they liked to sweeten their food with honey. The farm work was mainly done by slaves and the wealthy owners might only visit their country house occasionally. Not every Romano-British farm belonged to a rich landowner, though. There were lots of much smaller, poorer farms dotted around the countryside, too.

If you were Roman...

When you went to bed in Roman times you would sleep on a simple wooden bed and your mattress would be a cloth bag filled with hay, wool or feathers. You would need to light your way to bed using a pottery lamp filled with olive oil or melted fat.

To use this pottery oil lamp, a Roman lit a waxy cord called a wick which went in the hole and soaked up the olive oil or fat inside. ▶

In the house

Villas were built in a rectangular shape, with rooms facing an open courtyard. The grandest rooms were the ones on show to visitors. The level of luxury depended on how rich the owner was, but most British villas had underfloor heating to cope with cold winters. Slaves kept a fire burning to warm air that circulated under the floors.

Posh pictures

The grandest villas were decorated with wall paintings and mosaics on the floors. The mosaics were made from tiny squares of coloured stone and glass called *tesserae*, fitted together to make patterns and pictures. Proud villa-owners employed the best mosaic-maker they could afford to create mosaics.

Look!

Roman mosaic-makers created geometric patterns and pictures of gods, goddesses and animals. This mosaic design, dating from 300 CE, is part of the Museum of London's Roman dining room exhibit.

Visit a palace

In 1960 workmen were digging a trench in Fishbourne, West Sussex, when they unearthed the remains of a grand Roman palace built roughly around 75 CE. It is the biggest Roman palace so far discovered in Britain.

Grand living, Roman-style

Although only wall fragments and mosaics now remain, archaeologists have worked out that Fishbourne had over 100 rooms. Many of them led out to shady covered walkways lined with elegant pillars, overlooking a beautiful garden and with a view of the sea.

The rooms were all decorated differently, and the mosaics were of the finest quality. We don't know who lived in the palace but it must have been a very important person – perhaps a Roman governor or a local tribal leader.

A recreation of how Fishbourne would have looked in Roman times. ▼

The garden at Fishbourne included this outdoor eating area. Guests reclined on the stone benches. ▶

A Roman garden

The Romans introduced gardens to Britain, and Fishbourne had smart garden terraces where people could stroll or sit by fountains and pools. Expensive garden statues, perhaps brought by boat from Rome, lined some of the paths. At Fishbourne you can see how the ancient garden might have looked and even explore a reconstructed Roman potting shed.

If you were Roman...

If you had visited Fishbourne in Roman times it would probably have been rather like going to Buckingham Palace. You would have been ushered in by servants and asked to wait in an outer room until the owner was ready to see you.

Rich rooms

The palace was destroyed by fire around 300 CE, but we can imagine what the rooms looked like. The Romans didn't have much furniture – no stuffed armchairs, carpets or chests of drawers, for instance. Instead the palace would have had couches, simply-designed chairs and low tables, all made from the finest materials. Oil lamps were suspended from the ceiling or hung from stands to light up the palace in the evening.

Visit a town

The Romans introduced towns to Britain for the first time. The biggest one was Londinium, now called London, which became the country's most important port and a centre of Roman government.

In a Roman town

Roman towns such as Londinium had streets lined with houses, shops and workshops. There were temples, public bathhouses and theatres, too. If you wanted to visit the heart of a town and spot important citizens, you went to the forum. It was a large square where people met up and heard public announcements.

A museum model of the port in Londinium. ▼

Busy Londinium

Londinium was a busy port where ships arrived from around the Empire, bringing goods from abroad, such as olive oil, wine and pottery. They left carrying British goods such as wool and metals. Most of Roman Londinium is buried deep under the modern city, but some remains have been found, including Roman ships found buried in the Thames' river mud.

Shopping and snacking

Roman shops were open to the street like a market stall. The shop owner often lived in a flat above his shop. While out shopping, you might stop at a snack bar, where people stood at a counter with bowls of food on display. Here you could have a snack, such as cheese smothered in honey, or perhaps the ancient Roman version of a pork kebab.

Look!

When archaeologists found the remains of a wooden Roman ship near Blackfriars Bridge in London, they discovered a gold coin hidden under the mast for good luck. The coin had a picture on it of Fortuna, the goddess of luck, but the ship's luck seems to have run out when it collided with another ship and sank.

If you were Roman...

The Romans brought the idea of using coins as money to Roman Britain. On one side, your coins would have shown a picture of the Roman emperor who was ruling at the time the money was made.

Come to dinner

Dinner with a wealthy Roman meant you ate the best food served on the most stylish plates and bowls. Wealthy Romans ate different food to poorer people.

Dining with the wealthy

Well-off Romans ate food cooked by their slaves using expensive ingredients from abroad, such as spices, and a popular fish sauce called garum. When a Roman threw a banquet there were lots of courses designed to impress the guests, such as roast wild boar, swan or piglet. Guests lay on couches at banquets, propping themselves up on one elbow.

A grand Roman kitchen might have looked like this. ▼

If you were Roman...

Romans flavoured their food with herbs such as rosemary and thyme, never tried in Britain before. They also used herbs as medicine. If you had a headache they would give you mint tea, and if you ate too much and had tummy ache they would give you the herb chamomile.

Eating with the poor

Ordinary Celtic peasants didn't eat fine Roman cuisine. In the countryside they lived off stews and broths, bread and porridge made from what they could grow and gather in the countryside. Poor townsfolk often lived in cramped apartments with no way of cooking, so they bought food from taverns and snack bars.

Eating with soldiers

Writing found at the army base of Vindolanda (see p9) lists some of the food ordered for the soldiers there. The shopping list included beans, chickens, apples, eggs, fish sauce and olives. The soldiers ate lots of bread and bacon, too. In the army, every century (group of 80 soldiers) baked its own bread.

Look!

The army was split into small groups of eight soldiers that shared rooms and tents. Each group had a folding frying pan that they carried in their kit for cooking fry-ups! The folding frying pan shown below was used by soldiers at the fortress at Caerleon in Wales (see p6).

Take a bath

When Romans bathed they liked to meet their friends to chat and relax. Britain's Roman towns had public bathhouses where people could pay to bathe and exercise. Army bases had bathhouses for the soldiers to use.

▲ The Roman baths at Bath are now a museum.

At the bathhouse

A Roman bathhouse was rather like a modern spa. Visitors relaxed in rooms that were kept cold or warm, steamy or dry, and they could swim in cool or warm plunge pools. Some bathhouses had large swimming pools and exercise halls where visitors lifted weights or played ball games. It was possible to buy a snack, get a massage or even play gambling games.

Soap versus oil

The local Celts were noted for their cleanliness, and used soap made from animal fat mixed with ashes. The Romans preferred to smear themselves with olive oil scented with flowers. Then they sat sweating in a hot bathhouse room, before slaves scraped off the oil, dirt and sweat with a curved metal tool called a strigil (below).

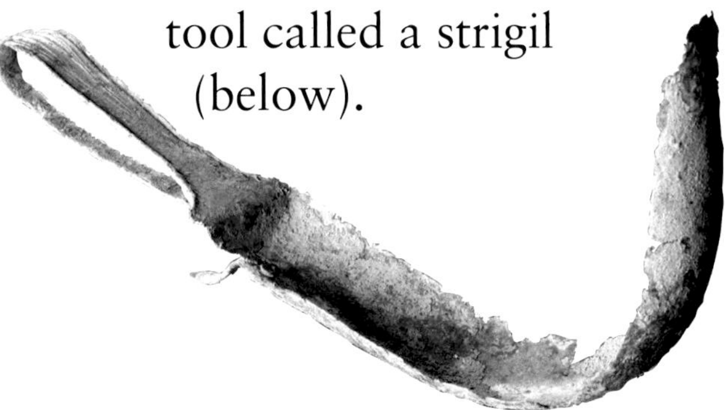

Look!

Excavations of Roman bath drains around Britain have uncovered lost jewellery, coins, bath equipment such a tweezers and oil flasks, and even the remains of food the bathers ate, such as animal bones and poppy seeds.

▲ Lost earrings such as this one have been rediscovered in drains.

The best baths

Aquae Sulis, now called Bath in Somerset, was a popular tourist destination for Romans because of its hot springs. A hot water swimming bath was built over the springs, as well as an important temple (see p26). Bathing there was not simply about getting clean. The Romans and the Celts alike believed that the spring waters were magical and could cure illnesses.

If you were Roman...

If you needed to go to the toilet in your home you would probably use a pot in the corner, to be emptied outside later. If you were out and about you could visit a public toilet block, where you would sit alongside other people chatting as you went to the toilet. Then you would use a sponge on a long stick for wiping yourself.

Dress to impress

We know what people wore in Roman Britain from pictures, statues and writing of the time, and from remains such as shoes, jewellery and hairpins.

Roman men

Romans in Britain wore much the same clothes as they did in other parts of the Empire, only with more woolly layers for the cold, wet weather. For everyday clothing men wore a tunic with a belt. In cold weather they added more layers, plus a cloak. They wore a toga – a large piece of cloth wrapped around the body – for official business.

If you were Roman...

If you were a woman living in Roman Britain you would follow the hair fashions that came from Rome, shown on coins and statues. Hair fashions were always changing, depending on what noble ladies were wearing back in Rome (see p23).

This model is wearing her hair in a style popular with wealthy Roman women. ▶

Look!

The Museum of London has an example of a very unusual piece of Roman clothing – a leather bikini bottom (shown right)! It's possible this might have been worn by an acrobat, but nobody knows for sure.

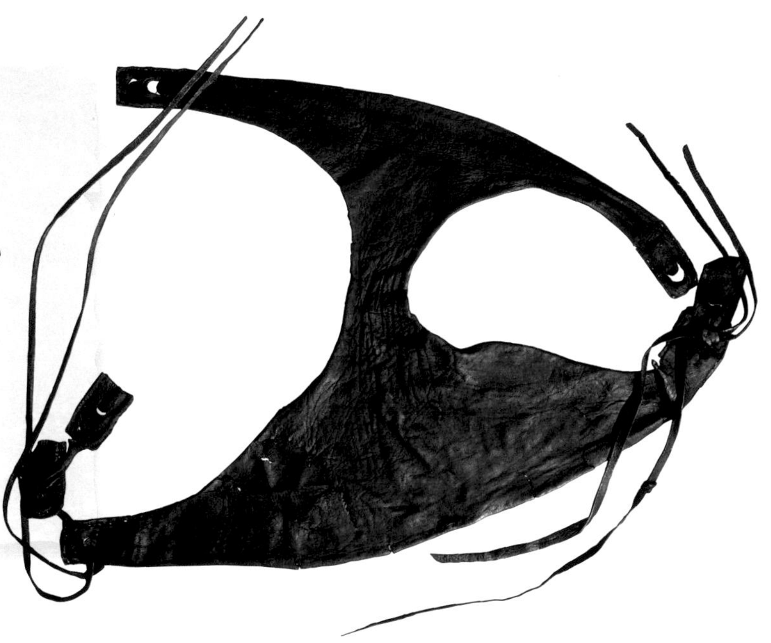

Roman women

Women wore ankle-length tunics with shorter tunics on top. They grew their hair long and pinned it up, sometimes in very complicated styles with hairpieces and even wire frames. They reddened their lips and cheeks and wore pale skin make-up made of chalk or lead. They used face ointments, too. A 2,000-year-old pot of ointment, discovered in London, contained moisturiser made from animal fat, starch and tin oxide, ingredients still used in modern make-up.

Lucky bling

It seems that the Romans liked to wear jewellery. Men wore rings and brooches to pin their clothes in place. Women liked necklaces, earrings and bracelets. Roman jewellery was often designed using symbols to bring good luck or to ward off 'the evil eye' (bad spells and curses). A snake-shaped bracelet was thought to ward off evil.

The ointment pot found in London in 2003. ▼

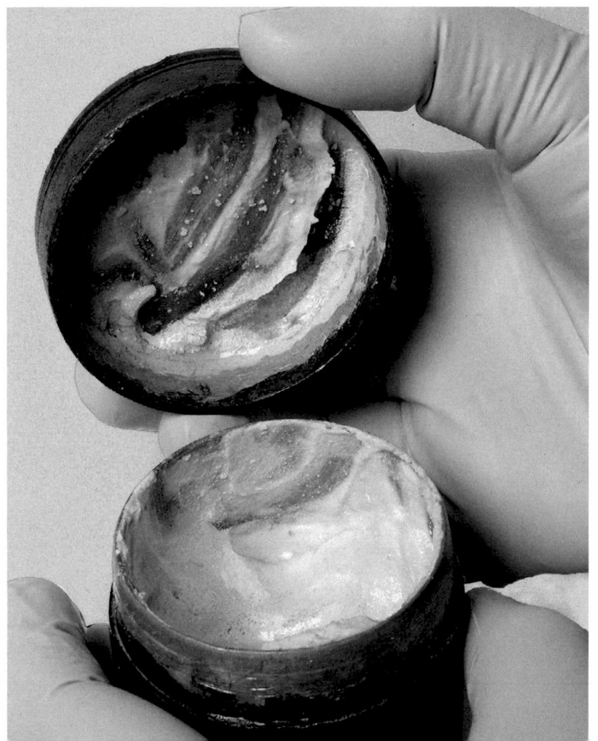

See a show

Many Roman towns had an amphitheatre – an open-air stadium where fans could see gladiator fights. Some towns also had theatres where plays were put on.

▲ Part of the ruins of Chester's amphitheatre are open to the public.

Look!

Roman actors wore masks to show the type of character they were playing – whether the character was good or bad, young or old, for instance. The pottery mask on the right may once have been worn by an actor, although nobody knows for sure. It was found near Warrington in Cheshire.

Chester's chains

You can see the remains of Chester's amphitheatre, which had room for a big crowd of around 7,000 spectators. They watched fights between gladiators and the staged hunting of captured animals, such as wild boars or bears.

There were probably boxing matches and wrestling matches, too. In the centre of Chester's amphitheatre there were blocks fitted with chains which may have been used to chain prisoners who were about to be executed in front of the crowds.

Give me good luck

Inside Chester amphitheatre archaeologists found a stone altar to the Greek goddess Nemesis. People believed she controlled people's fate and made sure that justice was done. Perhaps gladiators made an offering on the altar before they went out to fight.

Off to the theatre

As well as amphitheatres, a few Roman theatres have been found around Britain. Verulamium, now called St Alban's, still has its theatre remains, where the spectators sat in a semicircle to see the stage. Roman plays were lively comedies or violent tragedies with lots of deaths.

▲ Re-enactor gladiators stage a mock fight in Chester's amphitheatre.

If you were Roman...

If you went to see a show at Chester's amphitheatre you would be given a numbered token to help you find your seat. Outside you could buy snacks and souvenirs. We know this because a numbered token, cooked animal bones and souvenir pots with pictures of gladiators on them have all been found around the edges of the arena.

Visit a temple

The Romans believed in lots of deities (gods and goddesses) and made offerings to them. It was thought that the deities would send disasters if they were angry!

Druid destruction

When the Romans arrived in Britain they found the Celts worshipping their own gods and goddesses, thought to live in natural places such as lakes and streams. The Romans recognised these special places as sacred but they did not accept the local Celtic priests, called Druids. The Druids urged resistance against the invaders, so they were hunted down and destroyed by the Roman army.

Top temples

In Roman towns there were large temples dedicated to the most important deities. Inside these grand buildings there was usually a giant statue of a god or goddess. For instance, in the temple next to the baths at Aquae Sulis (now Bath, see p20), there was a giant statue of Sulis Minerva, goddess of healing and sacred springs. The head was rediscovered (left), still partly covered in gold

◀ The head of the statue of Sulis Minerva found at Bath.

leaf. The statue once glinted in the temple lamplight, towering impressively over visitors.

A new picture

When Roman emperors died they were declared gods and people were expected to worship them. However, in the 1st century CE visitors to Britain brought news of a new religion – Christianity – which did not allow for emperor-worship. The Romans banned it, imprisoning and sometimes executing anyone they found illegally praying to the Christian god. Christians had to worship in secret until 313 CE, when Emperor Constantine allowed them to worship freely.

Look!

The earliest known picture of Jesus found in Britain dates from the 4th century CE. It was part of a Roman mosaic found in the remains of a villa in Dorset. The head is in front of the Greek letters *chi* and *rho*, the first two letters of Christ's name.

Time to leave

By the 400s CE fighting was breaking out across the western part of the Roman Empire. Although Britannia was being raided by its neighbours, the Roman army was needed to protect other parts of the Empire.

Raiders all around

Raiders attacked the shores of Britain long before the Romans left, sailing in to steal what they could grab. The Roman army built a series of forts along the southern coast, manned by soldiers to keep watch and guide Roman ships to safety. You can visit some of the fort sites, such as Portchester Castle in Hampshire, and imagine being on guard, watching the sea for raiders.

A medieval castle was built inside the Roman walls of the fort at Portchester. ▼

Abandoned

The year 367 CE was a terrible one for Britannia. The best troops had already left and now attacks came from tribes in Ireland and Scotland, and from Saxons who sailed across the North Sea from the areas we now call Germany and Denmark. In 410 CE the last of the Roman soldiers left and the Britons were told to look after themselves. The invaders came pouring in, and though the Britons tried to fight back, they were eventually defeated.

New settlers

We don't know exactly what happened to all the ordinary Romano-British people living around the country. Some must have been killed in fighting and some may have become slaves. Others fled to Wales or across to Brittany (north-west France). The new Saxon settlers had a completely different lifestyle to the Romans, preferring to live in small farming villages. Roman buildings were left to crumble.

Look!

Around the time the Roman army left, someone buried thousands of gold and silver coins and precious objects in Hoxne, Suffolk. Perhaps the owner intended to come back when the danger had passed, but they never did. The rediscovered hoard, including this silver empress pepperpot, is now in the British Museum in London.

Glossary

Amphitheatre A Roman open-air stadium.

Aquae Sulis The Roman name for the town of Bath.

Auxiliary Someone in the Roman army who was not a Roman citizen.

Britannia The Roman name for Britain.

Camulodunum The Roman name for Colchester.

Celts Tribes who ruled southern Britain before the Romans came.

Centurion A Roman army officer.

Deities Gods and goddesses.

Druid A Celtic priest.

Forum A Roman town square.

Garum Fish sauce used in Roman food rather like one used in Thai cooking today.

Gladiator A trained performing fighter.

Londinium The Roman name for London.

Mosaic A picture made up of lots of tiny pieces fitted together.

Picts Tribes that lived in the far north of Britain.

Roman citizen Someone who had rights and was protected by Roman law.

Romano-British Local British people who lived like Romans.

Saxons People from the area we now call Germany.

Strigil A metal tool used for scraping oil off someone's skin in a Roman bathhouse.

Tesserae Tiny pieces of coloured stone or glass fitted together to make a picture on the floor.

Torc A necklace made of metal strands twisted together.

Verulamium The Roman name for St Alban's.

Villa A Roman country house.

Further information

Weblinks

http://www.museumoflondonimages.com
Go to the Roman section to see objects from Roman London.

http://www.britishmuseum.org/explore/young_explorers1.aspx
All sorts of activities based on the collections at the British Museum.

http://www.stalbansmuseums.org.uk/Your-Visit/Verulamium-Museum
The Museum of Everyday Life in Roman Britain, based in St Alban's.

https://www.museumwales.ac.uk/roman/
The website of the National Roman Legion Museum, in Caerleon, Wales.

Note to parents and teachers: Every effort has been made by the Publishers to ensure that the web sites in this book are suitable for children, that they are of the highest educational value, and that they contain no inappropriate or offensive material. However, because of the nature of the Internet, it is impossible to guarantee that the contents of these sites will not be altered. We strongly advise that Internet access is supervised by a responsible adult.

Timeline

43 CE The Roman army invades Britain.

49 CE Roman ex-soldiers found Camulodunum (Colchester). Briefly it is Britain's capital.

61 CE Some British tribes revolt, led by Boudica, but they are defeated in battle.

78 CE The Romans complete the conquering of Wales.

79 CE New government buildings are opened in St Alban's. It becomes an important town.

122 CE Emperor Hadrian orders the building of Hadrian's Wall.

211/212 CE Britain is divided into two provinces. Londinium (London) is the capital of the south and Eboracum (York) is the capital of the north.

250 CE Northern Scottish tribes called Picts, Scots (from Ireland), and people from the eastern coast of Germany begin to attack the British Isles.

306 CE After conflict between proposed emperors, the army in Britain hails Constantine as emperor.

314 CE Constantine declares an end to the persecution of Christians.

367 CE Attacks begin to overwhelm the frontiers of Roman Britain.

410 CE Roman troops leave Britain for good, and Britons are told to defend themselves.

Index